My DISNEY STARS AND HEROES 2

Student's Book with eBook

Viv Lambert and Cheryl Pelteret

Scope and Sequence

	Vocabulary	Grammar and communication	Personal and Social Skills	Cross-curricular	Project and strategies
1 **We are different** page 10 	**Adjectives** Appearance adjectives and nouns Abilities	Is she tall or short? She's tall. Does she have dark hair or red hair? She has dark hair. Does he have a beard? Yes, he does./No, he doesn't. **Ask and answer about what people can do** What can she do? She can horseback ride. She can't ride a scooter. Can she cook? Yes, she can. /No, she can't.	**Social awareness:** Understanding the feelings of others How do you feel?, It's OK. **Story:** Different is fun!	**Art:** Drawing faces chin, eyebrows, line, middle	**Project:** 'My friend' poster **Self-management:** What I know vs what I can ask I can ask … I know …
2 **At the ocean** page 22	**Ocean words 1** Ocean words 2 Beach items	What's that? It's a sea lion. What are those? They're sea lions. **Ask and answer about possessions** Is this our home? Yes, it is./No, it isn't. Are these their shells? Yes, they are./No, they aren't.	**Self-management:** Knowing when to ask for help alone, Can you help me, please? **Story:** The beach trip	**Life Science:** The awesome octopus change color, skin, suckers, weak	**Project:** My ocean scene **Presentation skills:** Speaking loudly and clearly Can you hear me?
3 **Around town** page 34 	**Things in the street** Places in town 1 Places in town 2	Is there a museum? Yes, there is./No, there isn't. Are there any trams? Yes, there are./No, there aren't. **Ask and answer about where things are** Where are they? They're in the bedroom. Where's the mall? It's across from the hotel.	**Self-management:** Persistence bored, Don't give up!, I can't stop now., tired **Story:** The treasure hunt	**Math:** 3D shapes in a city cube, cuboid, cylinder, pyramid	**Project:** My town poster **Self-management:** Sharing group tasks I can draw …, task
4 **Let's eat** page 46 	**Food 1** Food 2 Meals and food	He likes soup. She doesn't like soup. Does she like tomatoes? Yes, she does./No, she doesn't. **Order and offer food** What would you like? I'd like some cake, please. Would you like some soup? Yes, please./No, thank you.	**Self-awareness:** Self-appreciation I can … . I'm good at it! **Story:** Let's make some juice!	**Science:** Food groups carbohydrates, dairy, fats, fruit and vegetables, proteins	**Project:** My food menu **Presentation skills:** Good role-play behavior please, take turns, thank you
5 **The weather** page 58 	**Seasons** Weather Activities	What's the weather like? It's warm and sunny. It's very warm. **Ask and answer about seasonal activities** What do you do in winter? In winter, we play indoors.	**Relationship skills:** Listening to different ideas listen to ideas, that's a great idea, work together **Story:** The kite	**Life Science:** Ant life bark, nest, team, underground	**Project:** My activity tree **Self-management:** Following a plan check, make, show

Meet our Stars and Heroes!

1 🎧 0.1 💬 Listen and point. Then point and say.

Sticker time

2 Collect your friend at the start of each unit!

Cinderella (W)

Can: dance

Friends: birds and mice

Fergus (1)

Likes: animals

Lives: with his family

Dory (2)

Lives: in the ocean

Friends: Nemo and Marlin

Hiro (3)

Likes: robots

Family: aunt Cass, brother Tadashi

Tiana (4)

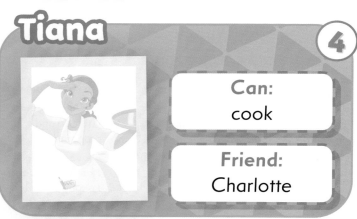

Can: cook

Friend: Charlotte

Atta (5)

Family: sister Dot

Friend: Flik

Bob (6)

Can: drive a car

Lives: with his family

Judy (7)

Job: police officer

Friend: Nick

Lilo (8)

Likes: music

Friend: Stitch

Olaf (9)

Likes: warm hugs

Friends: Anna and Elsa

Sing-along

3 🎵 **Listen, sing, and act.**

Hello, hello, everyone!
Welcome back!
Let's have some fun.
Friends and heroes everywhere.
Welcome back!
Let's have some fun!

4 ✏️ 💬 **Be a hero. Write, draw, and say.**

Name:
_____

I like _____
_____ .

I can _____
_____ .

My friends are
_____
_____ .

1 🎧 0.3 💬 **Listen, point, and say. Then ask and answer.**

What time is it?

It's two o'clock.

2 ▶ 0A **Watch the video. Check (✔). What time does Cinderella go home?**

1 three o'clock ◯   2 twelve o'clock ◯   3 eight o'clock ◯

3 🎧 0.4 ✏ **Listen and circle. Then draw.**

1 It's **eight** / **three** o'clock.

2 It's **ten** / **one** o'clock.

3 It's **five** / **nine** o'clock.

 I can ask and answer about the time.

1 Watch again. Are Cinderella's sisters nice?

2 Listen, point, and say. Then ask a friend.

20 twenty   **30** thirty   **40** forty   **50** fifty   **60** sixty

70 seventy   **80** eighty   **90** ninety   **100** a hundred

3 Listen and chant. ♩ ♩

4 Listen and color. Then play.

84   72   45   100   31   66

Purple.   Forty-five!   Talk buddies

 Collect your friend! page 4

I can say numbers 20–100.

1 🎧 0.8 💬 **Listen, point, and say. Then complete and ask a friend.**

Monday	Tuesday	Wednesday	Thursday	Friday	Saturday	Sunday

2 🎵 0.9 **Listen and chant.**

3 🎧 0.10 ✏️ **Listen and stick. Then write.**

Picture Dictionary page 118

Sticker time

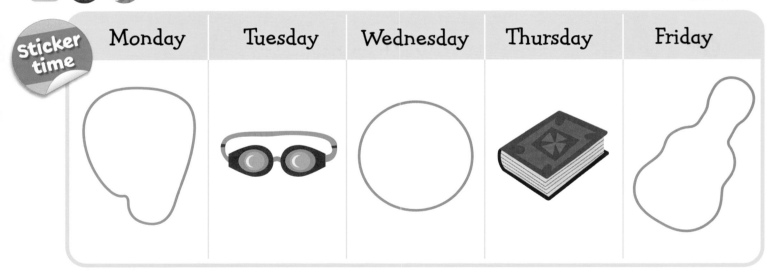

Monday	Tuesday	Wednesday	Thursday	Friday

❶ On _____ , I jump rope.   ❷ On _____ , I swim.

❸ On _____ , I play soccer.   ❹ On _____ , I play the guitar.

4 💬 **Ask and answer.**

What do you do on Saturdays?

On Saturdays, I play soccer.

Talk buddies

I can name the days of the week.

Nice to meet you!

1 🎧 0.11 **Listen and read. When does Amelia dance?**

① Hello. I'm Martina. I'm 26. I can play the guitar.

Hi. My name's Pedro. I'm ten. This is my sister.

② Hello! I'm Laura. I'm eight. I have 39 teddy bears!

Wow!

③ What's your name?

I'm Amelia. On Saturdays, I dance.

④ And I'm Niko! I swim before school on Mondays, Wednesdays, and Fridays! I get up at six o'clock.

Wow! Nice to meet you all!

Make new friends!

2 ✏️ **Write the numbers in words.**

8   6   10   26   39

1 Martina is _____ .

2 Laura is _____ .

3 Laura has _____ teddy bears.

4 Pedro is _____ .

5 Niko gets up at _____ o'clock.

3 ✏️💬 **Draw, write, and say.**

I'm _____ . On Mondays, I _____ .

Nice to meet you!

I can share personal information.

9

1 We are different

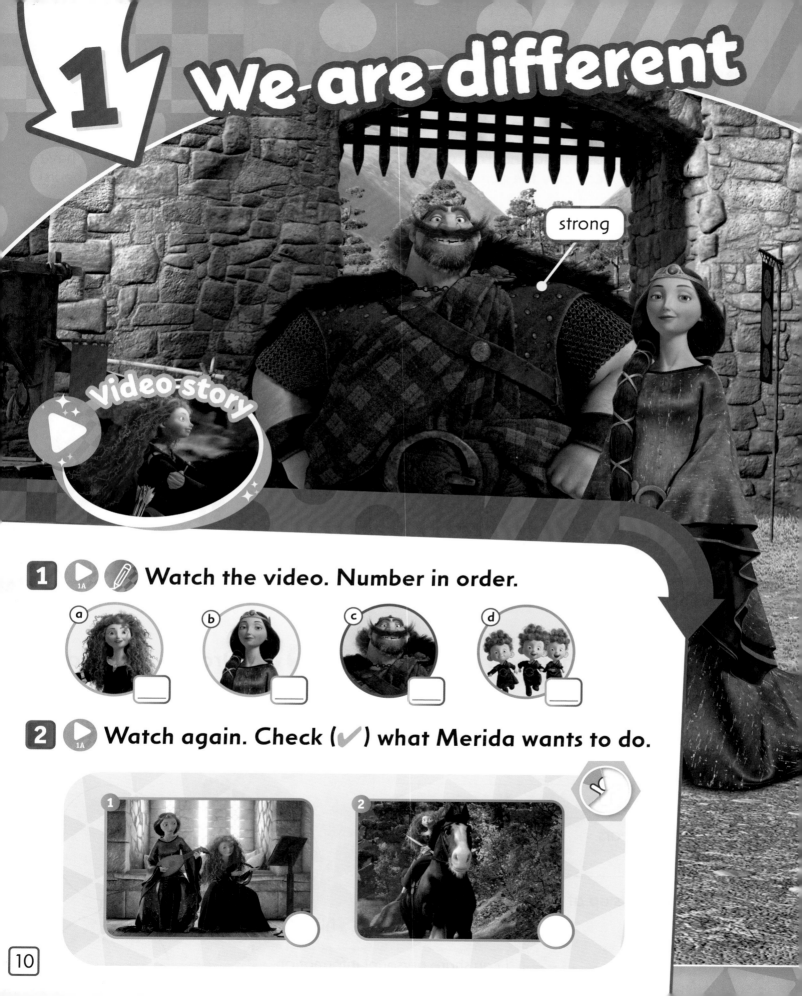

strong

Video-story

1 ▶ 🖉 Watch the video. Number in order.

a
b
c
d

2 ▶ Watch again. Check (✔) what Merida wants to do.

1

2

3 🎧 💬 **Listen, find, and say. Then ask a friend.**

4 🎵 **Listen, chant, and act.**

fast

tall

short

I can describe people.

Collect
your friend!
page 4

1  **Listen, point, and say. Then play.**

Eight.   Beard!

1 dark

2 blond

3 gray

4 straight

5 curly

6 long

7 glasses

8 beard

2 **Listen and stick. Then play *Guess who?***

Sticker time

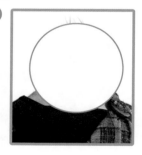
1

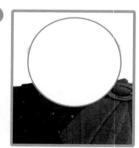
2

3

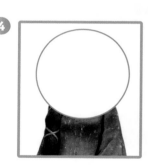
4

3 **Read and circle for you. Then draw and tell a friend.**

1 I have **long** / **short** hair.

2 It's **blond** / **dark** / **red**.

3 It's **curly** / **straight**.

4 I **have** / **don't have** glasses.

Talk buddies

I have …

I can describe appearance.

1 🎧 1.5 **Listen and check (✔).**

🎧 1.6

Is she tall or short?
She's tall.
Does she have dark hair or red hair?
She has dark hair.
Does he have a beard?
Yes, he does./
No, he doesn't.

2 🎧 1.7 **Listen and say *Yes* or *No*.**

1

Grandpa

2
Mom

3

Billy

4

Betty

3 💬 **Cover the pictures in 2. Ask and answer.**

Does Grandpa have short hair or long hair?   He has short hair.

Does he have glasses?   No, he doesn't.

Talk buddies

I can ask and answer about appearance.

13

Different is fun!

1 🎧 1.8 **Listen and read. What color hair does Daisy have?**

① Look! There's Amelia.

② Where's Daisy?

③ Are you OK, Daisy? Where's your picture?

It's here, but … only I have red hair.

④ But different is fun, Daisy! Look! Only Laura is tall.

Yes! And only Amelia has glasses.

⑤ Look! Daisy has red hair. And now I have red hair!

It's curly too!

Spot!
Who has a beard?

⑥ Laura has long red hair!

Amelia has short red hair!

Smile!

14

⑦

Oh! We all have red hair. We all look the same.

Amelia's right. Different is fun! Here's my picture.

The end

2 ✏️ Read and circle.

① Does Amelia have long or short red hair?   She has **long** / **short** hair.

② Is Laura tall or short?   She's **tall** / **short**.

③ Who has glasses?   **Daisy** / **Amelia** has glasses.

④ How many children have red hair at the end?   **Three**. / **Seven**.

3 Read and check (✔).

① How does Daisy feel at the beginning?

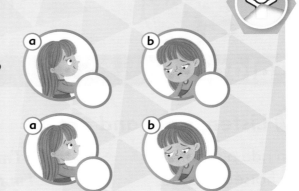
ⓐ   ⓑ

② How does Daisy feel at the end?

ⓐ   ⓑ

4 💬 Act out the story.

Look! Only Laura is tall.

Talk buddies

Yes! And only Amelia has glasses.

I can read and understand a story.

1 🎧 1.9 💬 **Listen, point, and say. Then play.**

1 cook

2 horseback ride

3 play basketball

4 play the drums

5 take pictures

6 ride a scooter

📖 **Think and draw.**

the drums

play

the guitar   soccer

Picture Dictionary
page 119

2 🎧 1.10 💬 **Listen and say. Then play in pairs.**

Take pictures!

Sing-along

3 🎵 1.11 **Listen, sing, and act.**

I can ride a scooter.
I can horseback ride.
But I can't play basketball
And I can't ride a bike.

I'm not very tall.
I'm not very strong.
There are some things I can't do,
but I can sing this song!
I can sing this song, I can sing this song.
I can sing this song, I can sing this song.

I can take pictures.
I can jump and run.
But I can't cook a pizza
And I can't play the drums.

Chorus

I can name free time activities.

Extra Lesson >>>>>>>>

Go online
Phonics

1 ▶ 1B **Watch the video. Check (✔). What can Merida do?**

fly ◯   horseback ride ◯   climb ◯

 1.12
What can she do?
She can horseback ride.
She can't ride a scooter.
Can she cook?
Yes, she can./No, she can't.

2 ✏️ 💬 **Look, read, and write *Yes* or *No*. Then play in pairs.**

Eva can ride a scooter.   Yes!

Eva

Chris

1 Eva can ride a scooter. _____

2 Eva can draw. _____

3 Eva can't dance. _____

4 Chris can't play basketball. _____

5 Chris can cook. _____

6 Chris can run fast. _____

Let's communicate!

3 💬 **Use the cut outs. Play the game.**

 cut outs

 Hassan

 Adam

Is it a girl or a boy?   It's a boy.

Can he cook?   No, he can't.

I can ask and answer about what people can do.

♫ 1.13 Listen and sing.

Understanding others' feelings

♫ I ask *How are you?*
Do you feel ok?
Are you happy or sad?
Do you want to play?

We're working hard,
We keep trying!
We are heroes,
We are heroes!

We're dreaming big,
We don't give up!
We are heroes,
We are heroes!

♫ I talk to my friends,
Say *I'm here for you.*
Smile at them
and watch them smile, too.

♫ *Chorus*

1 Look and number. How do they feel?

 a

 b

 c

 d

1 happy
2 angry
3 excited
4 sad

2 1.14 Listen and check (✔). Why do they feel this way?

1 a  b

2 a  b

3 a b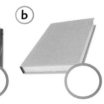

3 Look and circle. How does your friend feel today?

 angry

 sad

 happy

 excited

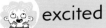 worried

 **Be a hero!**

 Use your eyes and ears to understand your friends' feelings.

Social awareness I can say how someone feels.

Drawing faces

Learn to draw faces!
Use a pencil, a ruler, and an eraser.

1 **Let's explore!** Listen, read, and number.

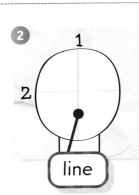 chin

 line

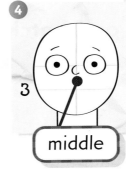 eyebrows

 middle

a Draw the eyes on line 2. Now draw the **eyebrows**. ☐

b Draw a circle. Then draw the **chin**. Use your eraser! ☐

c Draw the nose in the **middle** of line 1, and then draw line 3 like this →. ☐

d Draw the mouth on line 3. Now draw the hair and ears. ☐

e Draw two lines: **line** 1 like this ↑ and line 2 like this →. ☐

2 💡 **Think** Look and put a ✔ or ✘. Is it OK?

1. chin ◯
2. ears ◯
3. eyes ◯
4. eyebrows ◯
5. mouth ◯
6. nose ◯

3 🖊 **Do** Look and say. Then draw one more. How can you show feelings?

 1

 2

 3

Number 1 is sad.

I can read and understand about how to draw a face.

'My friend' poster

Self-management

Let's review

1 ✏️ **Read and match.**

❶

❷

ⓐ My friend has black hair. He can horseback ride and play soccer.

ⓑ My friend has curly hair. He can't play soccer, but he can play basketball.

Get ready

2 🎧 1.16 **Listen and check (✔) what Cleo knows about her friend.**

She has blond hair. ◯

She can dance. ◯

She has blue eyes. ◯

She can ride a scooter. ◯

Workbook page 13

Create

3 🎨 **Now make your poster. Write.**

Reflect 🙁 🙂 😀

4 **How did I do?**

I ask my friend. ◯

I write about my friend. ◯

I make my poster. ◯

I can make a poster and describe my friend.

I can do it!

1 🖉 💬 **Read and number. Then ask and answer.**

1 She has long red hair.

2 He's tall. He's strong.

3 She's tall. She has straight hair.

4 He has short curly hair.

Is Merida's mom short or tall?

2 🖉 **Look and write can or can't. Then draw and say for you.**

	🛴	🥁	🏀	📷	🍲
Asta	🙁	🙂	🙁	🙁	🙂
You					

1 Asta _____ ride a scooter.

2 She _____ play the drums.

3 She _____ play basketball.

4 She _____ take pictures.

5 She _____ cook.

3 💡 **Think and check (✔). Then stick!**

I can ...

💬 describe people ☐

📖 read a story ☐

🎵 sing a song ☐

🧍 understand my friends' feelings ☐

Sticker time

☑ **I completed Unit 1!**

2 At the ocean

ocean

shark

Video-story

1 ▶ **2A** Watch the video. Check (✔). Who does Dory want to find?

2  **Watch again. Number in order. Who does Dory ask for help?**

a

b

c

3 **Listen, find, and say. Then ask a friend.**

4 **Listen, chant, and act.**

octopus

boat

PA 1200 CF | 580

I can name ocean words.

Collect your friend!

?

page 4

1 🎧 2.3 💬 **Listen, point, and say. Then play.**

1 starfish

2 sea lion

3 shell

4 whale

5 dolphin

6 crab

7 jellyfish

8 beach

2 🎧 2.4 ✏️ **Listen and stick. Then circle and say.**

Sticker time

1 There's a **crab** / **jellyfish** on the beach.

2 There's a **sea lion** / **dolphin** under the boat.

3 There are three **whales** / **sharks**.

4 There are people **on the beach** / **in the boat**.

3 💬 **Cover the picture in 2. Ask and answer.**

Where's the sea lion?

It's on the rock.

Talk buddies

I can name ocean animals and things on the beach.

1 🎧 2.5 ✏️ **Who's Gerald? Listen and check (✔). Then circle.**

🎧 2.6
What's that?
It's a sea lion.
What are those?
They're sea lions.

They're / It's sea lions.

2 ✏️ **Read and circle. Then write.**

1

What's **this / that**?
It's a _____ .

2

What are **these / those**?
They're _____ .

3

What are **these /
those**?
_____

4

What's **this / that**?
_____

3 💬 **Point, ask, and answer.**

What's that?

It's a whale.

Talk buddies

I can ask and answer about what things are.

The beach trip

1 🎧 2.7 **Listen and read. Which animals do the children help?**

① Oh, no! Look at the beach!

② Are these shells?

No, they're crabs. Look! They have legs. They can run.

③ And what's that?

It's a starfish.

Oh, no! Poor starfish! It can't move.

④ Come and play in the ocean!

You go, Amelia. I can help this starfish alone.

⑤ Later … I'm tired now. Can you help me?

Yes, of course. But the beach is big.

Wait! I have an idea.

⑥ Help us clean the beach.

LUIZA

There! Help us clean the beach.

Spot!
Can you find a dolphin?

⑦ Wow! Thanks, everyone.

The animals are happy now.

The end

2 ✏️ Look, read, and write.

| bag | beach | crabs | ocean | starfish |

❶ The _____ can run.

❷ The _____ can't move.

❸ The starfish is in the _____ .

❹ Niko wants to play in the _____ .

❺ The children clean the _____ .

3 ✏️ Read and circle.

Pedro **can** / **can't** do it alone.

Pedro **can** / **can't** do it alone.

4 💬 Act out the story.

But the beach is big.

Wait! I have an idea.

Talk buddies

I can read and understand a story.

1 Listen, point, and say. Then play.

1 bucket

2 towel

3 umbrella

4 sunhat

5 sandcastle

6 surfboard

In the ocean or on the beach?

on the beach
towel
surfboard
shark
in the ocean

Picture Dictionary
page 120

2 Look at 1. Listen and say *Yes* or *No*. Then play in pairs.

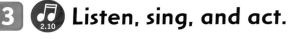
The bucket is blue.

No!

Sing-along

3 Listen, sing, and act.

*Let's go to the beach today
Make a sandcastle, swim, and play!*

Is this your umbrella?
Yes, it is. It's our umbrella.

*Let's go to the beach today
Put a sunhat on, swim, and play!*

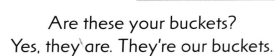

Are these your buckets?
Yes, they are. They're our buckets.

*Let's go to the beach today
Take a surfboard out, swim, and play!*

Is this your towel?
Yes, it is. It's our towel.

*Let's go to the beach today
Make a sandcastle, swim, and play!*

I can name things on the beach.

Extra Lesson

Go online
Phonics

1 **Watch the video. Circle. What does Dory remember about her home?**

rocks   shells   boats

2.11
Is this our home?
Yes, it is./No, it isn't.
Are these their shells?
Yes, they are./No, they aren't.

2 2.12 **Listen and put a ✔ or ✖. Then circle and ask a friend.**

1 ❶ Jacob and Isa have a boat.

Is that **our** / **their** boat?

❸ Where are our buckets?

Are those **our** / **their** buckets?

❷ We have an umbrella.

Is that **our** / **their** umbrella?

❹ Where are their surfboards?

Are those **our** / **their** surfboards?

Let's communicate!

3 **Use the cut outs. Play the game.**

 Cut outs

 Are these our buckets?

 Yes, they are.

I can ask and answer about possessions.

♪ 1.13
♬ Listen and sing. ♬

Asking for help

1 Check (✔) when Dory and Pedro ask for help.

2 🎧 2.13 ✏️ Listen and number. Then read and check (✔).

1 Can you help me, please? ◯

2 Can I do it, please? ◯

3 💡 ✏️ Circle the good ways to ask for help.

Get angry.

Cry.

Ask a friend.

Say *please* and *thank you*.

Say what help I need.

Yell.

Help

⭐ Be a hero! ⭐

Who can you ask for help? Make a "Helping Heroes" list.

Self-management I can ask for help.

The awesome octopus

1 🎧 2.14 **Let's explore!** Listen and read.
Why does an octopus change color?

suckers

The octopus is great at hiding. Its **skin** can **change color**. It can turn blue, gray, or green. Other animals can't see it, so they can't eat it.

The octopus has eight arms. Its arms aren't **weak**. They're very strong and they have **suckers** on them. The octopus can open shells with its arms.

The octopus doesn't have bones. Its body is soft, so it can hide in very small places.

2 💡 **Think** Read and circle.

❶ The octopus can change its **skin** / **shell** color.

❷ The octopus has **strong bones** / **a soft body**.

❸ The octopus uses its arms to **open** / **close** shells.

3 ✏️ **Do** Look and write.

arms ~~bones~~ ~~eyes~~ fingers
legs skin suckers

octopus   **me**

eyes   bones

I can read and understand about the octopus.

31

My ocean scene

Let's review

1 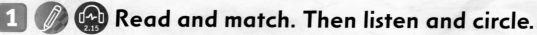 **Read and match. Then listen and circle.**

1

a There are crabs on the beach.

b There's a jellyfish in the ocean.

2

Get ready

2 2.16 **Listen and check (✔). What does Lena do this time?**

She takes a deep breath. ◯

She sits down. ◯

She speaks loudly. ◯

She speaks clearly. ◯

Workbook page 25

Create

3 🎨 💬 **Now make your ocean scene. Then tell the class.**

Reflect ☹ 🙂 😄

4 **How did I do?**

I speak loudly. ◯

I speak clearly. ◯

I present my project. ◯

I can make and present an ocean scene.

I can do it!

1 ✏️ 💬 **Look, read, and number. Then ask and answer.**

1 octopus
2 sea lion
3 bucket
4 shell
5 boat
6 umbrella
7 shark
8 sandcastle

2 ✏️ **Read and circle.**

1 What's **that** / **those**? It's a house.

2 Do Dory's parents live here?

Is it **our** / **their** house?

3 What are **that** / **those**? They're turtles.

4 Look at the turtles! Dory and Nemo are **our** / **their** friends.

3 💡 **Think and check (✔). Then stick!**

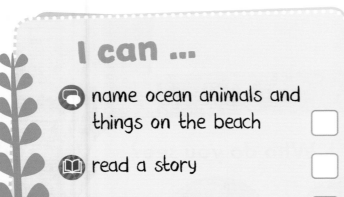

I can ...

💬 name ocean animals and things on the beach ☐

📖 read a story ☐

🎵 sing a song ☐

👐 ask for help ☐

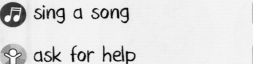

Sticker time

✔️ **I completed Unit 2!**

3 Around town

Video-story

1 ▶ 3A **Watch the video. Check (✔). Who do you see?**

2 ▶ **Watch again. Check (✔). What do Tadashi and Hiro say when they're tired?**

I can do this. ◯   I can stop now. ◯

I can't do this. ◯   I can't stop now. ◯

3 🎧 💬 **Listen, point, and say. Then ask a friend.**

1 street   2 truck   3 tram   4 bus

4 🎵 **Listen, chant, and act.**

I can name things on the street.

Collect your friend!
?
page 4

1 🎧 3.3 💬 Listen, point, and say. Then play.

1 grocery store

2 train station

3 museum

4 movie theater

5 bookstore

6 hospital

7 restaurant

8 fire station

2 🎧 3.4 ✏️ Listen and number.

Green Street

3 ✏️ Look at 2. Find and circle five differences.

Blue Street

4 💬 Play the game.

There's a train station.

Blue Street.

Talk buddies

I can name places in town.

1 🎧 3.5 ✏️ **Listen and circle.**

Are there any red buses?

Yes, there are. / No, there aren't.

🎧 3.6

Is there a museum?
Yes, there is./No, there isn't.
Are there any trams?
Yes, there are./No, there aren't.

2 🎧 3.7 💬 **Listen and stick. Then ask and answer.**

1

Sticker time

Newtown

2

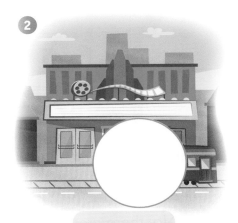

Freetown

3

Townsville

3 💬 **Ask and answer questions about your town.**

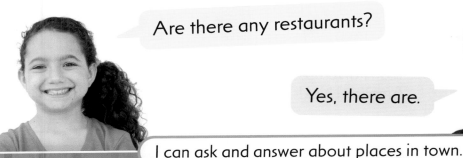

Are there any restaurants?

Yes, there are.

Talk buddies

I can ask and answer about places in town.

The treasure hunt

1 🎧 3.8 **Listen and read. Where are the dinosaurs?**

Listen to this clue. It's a station, but you can't see a train here.

① I know! Fire station!

Let's go!

② OK, clue two. There's food here.

Grocery store?

There isn't a grocery store here, but there's a restaurant! Come on!

③ Oh! Niko and Laura are already here. I'm tired.

Come on, Pedro. We can do it! What's the clue?

④ You can see dinosaurs here.

Ah! There are dinosaurs at the museum. Let's go!

⑤ Are there any clues here?

No, there aren't.

I'm bored now.

Don't give up, Amelia. Think!

⑥ I know! The movie theater!

Quick! Run!

Spot!

Can you find two trucks?

⑦ Good job, Amelia. Good job, Pedro. These are for you!

Oh, wow! Thanks, Dad!

The end

2 Put a ✔ or ✗. Where do Pedro and Amelia go?

① MOVIES ② GROCERY STORE ③ MUSEUM ④ Restaurant ⑤ FIRE STATION

3 ✏️ **Read and number. What do they say?**

ⓐ I'm tired. ☐

ⓑ I'm bored. ☐

ⓒ We can do it. ☐

ⓓ Don't give up! ☐

4 💬 **Act out the story.**

I'm bored now.

Don't give up!

Talk buddies

I can read and understand a story.

1 🎧 3.9 💬 **Listen, point, and say. Then play.**

1 sports center

2 apartment building

3 hotel

4 mall

5 factory

6 police station

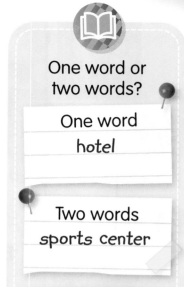

📖 **One word or two words?**

One word
hotel

Two words
sports center

Picture Dictionary
page 121

2 🎧 3.10 💬 **Listen and say. Then play in pairs.**

Hotel!

Sing-along

3 🎵 3.11 **Listen, sing, and act.**

Look at us! We're on the school bus.
Wave at us! We're on the yellow bus!

That's our apartment building. It's very tall.
There's the sports center, there's the mall.

Chorus

There's the police station, the hotel, too.
That's the factory. It's big and new.

Chorus

There's the fire station, see the red trucks.
Oh! Here's our school! Please stop the bus!

Chorus

I can name places in town.

》》Extra Lesson》》》》》》

Go online
Phonics

1 Watch the video. Check (✔). Where's Hiro?

kitchen ◯

bedroom ◯

living room ◯

Where is he?
He's between the bed and the chair.
Where are they?
They're in the bedroom.
Where's the mall?
It's across from the hotel.

2 Listen and number. Then ask and answer.

Where's the hospital?

1 movie theater   **2** sports center   **3** bookstore

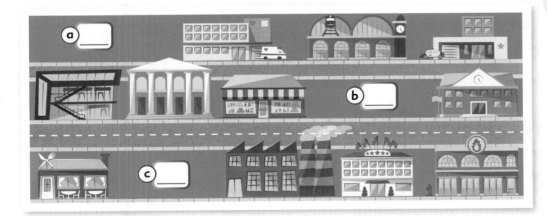

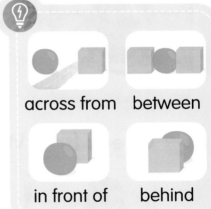

across from   between

in front of   behind

Let's communicate!

3 Use the cut outs. Play the game.

Where's the school?

It's across from the train station.

Cut outs

I can ask and answer about where things are.

1.13
Listen and sing.

Keep trying!

1 💬 Look and say. What is hard for them?

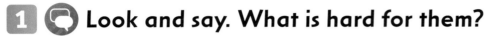

2 🎧 3.14 💬 Listen, check (✔), and say.

I can't do it. I'm tired. ◯

I can do it. I can't stop now. ◯

We can't find it. Let's go home. ◯

Don't give up. Let's look at the map. ◯

3 Check (✔). When do you feel tired or bored?

⭐ Be a hero! ⭐

Give yourself points for every hard thing you do this week!

4 💡 ✏️ Circle. What can you say to keep trying?

I'm bored.

I can do it.

I can't do it.

Don't give up.

Self-management   I can keep trying.

3D shapes in a city

1   **Let's explore!** Listen, read, and number.

a This house is a **cube**. All the sides are the same. They're square. ☐

d  **Cylinders** are tall circles. This hotel is in a very tall cylinder. The bedrooms aren't square! ☐

b There are a lot of shapes in towns and cities. This is a **pyramid**. Its sides are four triangles. ☐

c Some apartment buildings are **cuboids**. Their sides are rectangles. Some are tall, and some are short. This apartment building is a big cuboid. ☐

2  **Think** Read and write.

cube   cuboid   cylinder   pyramid

1. You can find triangle shapes in a _____ .

3. A _____ has rectangle sides.

2. A _____ is a tall circle.

4. Six squares make a _____ . All the sides are the same.

3 **Do** Count and write.

cylinders ☐   cuboids ☐

cubes ☐   pyramids ☐

I can read and understand about 3D shapes.

My town poster

Self-management

1 ✏️ **Look and write.**

❶ The hospital is between the hotel and the

_____ .

❷ The museum is _____ the hotel.

❸ The mall is _____ the hospital.

❹ The school is _____ the sports center.

2 🎧 ✏️ **Listen and match.**
3.16

❶ Eve   ⓐ sports center and hotel

❷ Lin   ⓑ hospital and train station

❸ Cam   ⓒ museum and school

Workbook page 37

3 🎨 **Now make your poster.
Write.**

4 How did I do?

I share group tasks.

I do my task.

I create my poster.

I can make a poster and write about my town.

I can do it!

1 3.17 **Look and write. Then listen and number.**

factory   police station   restaurant   tram

a

b

c

d

_____   _____   _____   _____

2 **Look and draw. Then ask your friend.**

Is there a hotel?

3 **Think and check (✓). Then stick!**

I can ...

 name places in town

read a story

sing a song

keep trying

Sticker time

✓ I completed **Unit 3!**

Go online
Big Project

4 Let's eat

peas

potatoes

cake

Video story

1 Watch the video. Check (✔). What do you see?

2  **Watch again. Circle. What can Tiana do?**

3 Listen, find, and say. Then ask a friend.

4 Listen, chant, and act.

soup

I can name food.

Collect your friend!
page 4

1 🎧 (4.3) 💬 **Listen, point, and say. Then play.**

1 lemons

2 kiwis

3 nuts

4 chocolate

5 chicken

6 mangoes

7 pineapples

8 yogurt

2 🎧 (4.4) 💬 **Listen and say. Then play.**

They're small and yellow.

Lemons!

3 ✏️ **Look and write.**

2 _____
4 _____
1 _____
3 _____

4 💬 **Play the game.**

I have lemons and mangoes.

I have lemons, mangoes, and chicken.

I have lemons.

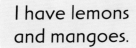

Talk buddies

I can name food.

1 🎧 4.5 ✏️ **Listen and circle.**

🎧 4.6

He likes soup.
He loves yogurt.
She doesn't like soup.
Does she like tomatoes?
Yes, she does./
No, she doesn't.

Tiana **likes** / **doesn't like** soup.

2 🎧 4.7 ✏️ **Listen and stick. Then write.**

Sticker time

ⓐ He _____ kiwis.
ⓑ He _____ lemons.

ⓐ She _____ peas.
ⓑ She _____ chocolate.

3 💬 **Look at 2. Play the game.**

He likes lemons.

No, he doesn't!

Talk buddies

I can say what people like and don't like.

Let's make some juice!

1 🎧 4.8 **Listen and read. What can Niko do?**

① Wow, Will! Your cookies are great!

Thanks. I can't cook, but I *can* make cookies!

Yum!

Pedro likes chocolate!

② Pedro, can you draw kiwis and lemons?

Yes! I can draw juice and cookies, too.

③ Hey, Niko! Come and help us.

Sorry! I can't help you. I can't draw and I can't cook!

④ Does Oscar like pineapples?

Yes, he does. He likes kiwis, mangoes, and bananas, too. He doesn't like lemons.

⑤ Oh, no! We need a new blender.

I can help. I can ride a bike fast!

Spot!
How many lemons can you find?

⑥ Ten minutes later …

Good job, Niko! Thank you!

You're welcome!

The end

2 ✏️ Read and write *Yes or No.*

1. Will has lemon cookies. _____
2. Pedro likes chocolate. _____
3. Laura makes juice. _____
4. Oscar likes lemons. _____

3 ✏️ Read and write. What can they do?

I can make _____ .

I can _____ .

I can _____ fast.

We can make _____ .

4 💬 Act out the story.

Wow, Will! Your cookies are great!

Thanks.

Talk buddies

I can read and understand a story.

1  Listen, point, and say. Then play.

1 breakfast ○

2 lunch ○

3 dinner ○

4 cereal ○

5 burger ○

6 fries ○

Draw times for you.

breakfast

Picture Dictionary
page 122

2 Listen and check (✔) in 1. Then ask and answer.

What time do you have breakfast?

I have breakfast at eight o'clock.

Sing-along

3  Listen, sing, and act.

I'm hungry. What's for breakfast?
I'm hungry. What's for lunch?
I'm hungry. What's for dinner?
I'm hungry. Munch, munch, munch!

Yogurt and cereal. That's breakfast.
Bread and jam. That's lunch!
Burger and fries. That's dinner.
Now some chocolate. Munch, munch, munch!

I'm hungry. What's for breakfast?
I'm hungry. What's for lunch?
I'm hungry. What's for dinner?
I'm hungry. Munch, munch, munch!

I can name food and meals. ≫Extra Lesson≫≫≫≫

Go online Phonics

1 Watch the video. Circle. What would Mr. La Bouff like?

pizza   cake   burger and fries

4.12
What would you like?
I'd like some cake, please.
Would you like some soup?
Yes, please./No, thank you.

2 4.13 Listen and match. Then play.

1

Aisha

2

Juan

3

Matt

Would you like some chicken?

Yes, please.

You're Juan!

Let's communicate!

3 Use the cut outs. Play the game.

Cut outs

Would you like some yogurt for breakfast?

No, thank you.

I can ask and answer about what food I would like.

1.13
Listen and sing.

Recognizing strengths

1 🖊 **Look and match. What can they do?**

 1

 2

 3

 4

 a

 b

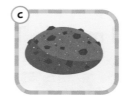 c

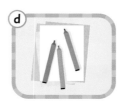 d

2 🎧 4.14 🖊 **Listen and check (✔). Then write for George.**

 1

 2

 3

I can _____
_____ .
I'm good at it.

3 💡 🖊 **Choose and write or think of your own ideas.**

I'm _____
_____ .
I can _____
_____ .

a good friend

kind   funny

draw   sing

cook

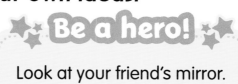
⭐ **Be a hero!** ⭐

Look at your friend's mirror. Say something nice about your friend.

You can make great cookies.

Self-awareness I can say what I'm good at.

Food groups

1 🎧 4.15 ✏️ **Let's explore! Listen, read, and match.**

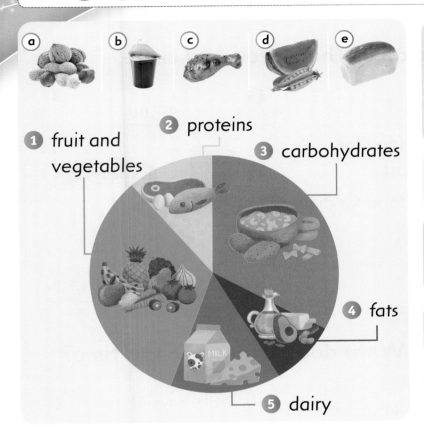

ⓐ ⓑ ⓒ ⓓ ⓔ

1 fruit and vegetables
2 proteins
3 carbohydrates
4 fats
5 dairy

Fruit and vegetables: Eat five different fruit and vegetables every day. You can eat tomatoes, pineapples, and peas. They have a lot of good things in them.

Proteins: Eat meat, fish, and eggs for strong muscles.

Carbohydrates: Do you play sports? Eat bread, potatoes, and noodles to have energy.

Fats: Some fats are good for you. Nuts have good fats.

Dairy: Milk, yogurt, and cheese give you strong bones.

2 💡 ✏️ **Think Read and circle. Then write one more.**

1 Fats: **fruit** / **nuts**

2 Carbohydrates: **milk** / **rice** and _____

3 Dairy: **eggs** / **cheese** and _____

4 Fruit and vegetables: **onions** / **cake** and _____

5 Proteins: **chicken** / **potatoes** and _____

3 ✏️ 💬 **Do Draw your favorite dinner. Say the food groups.**

I can read and understand about food groups.

My food menu

Let's review

1 **Look, read, and match. Then listen and circle.**

1

ⓐ This is food for breakfast.

ⓑ This is food for dinner.

2

Get ready

2 🎧 **4.17 Listen and check (✔). What does Marina do this time?**

She listens to her friend. ◯

She takes turns. ◯

She says *please* and *thank you*. ◯

Workbook page 49

Create

3 🎨 💬 **Now make your menu. Then act out with a friend.**

What would you like?

I'd like a pizza, please.

Reflect ☹ 🙂 😄

4 **How did I do?**

I make my project. ◯

I listen to my friend. ◯

I take turns. ◯

I say *please* and *thank you.* ◯

I can make a menu and act out a scene.

I can do it!

1 🎧 4.18 💬 **Listen and put a ✔ or ✘. Then say.**

1 2 3 4 5

She likes pineapples.

6 7 8 9

She doesn't like lemons.

2 ✏️ 🎧 4.19 **Read and write. Then listen and check.**

like   please   thank you   would

1 Good afternoon. What _____ you like?

2 I'd like some soup, _____ .

3 Would you _____ some bread?

4 No, _____ .

3 💡 **Think and check (✔). Then stick!**

I can ...

💬 name food items ☐

📖 read a story ☐

🎵 sing a song ☐

🌱 name my strengths ☐

.... ⚡ ....

Sticker time

✔ **I completed Unit 4!**

Test your progress with English Benchmark Young Learners

5 The weather

Video-story

summer

fall

spring

1 ▶ 5A **Watch the video. Check (✔) the animals you see.**

2 ▶ 5A **Watch again. Circle. Who likes Flik's ideas?**

Atta   Dot

3 🎧 5.1 💬 **Listen, find, and say. Then ask a friend.**

4 🎵 5.2 **Listen, chant, and act.**

winter

I can name the seasons.

Collect your friend! ? page 4

1 Listen, point, and say. Then play.

1 sunny

2 rainy

3 windy

4 snowy

5 cloudy

6 stormy

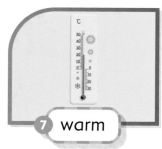
7 warm

8 cool

2 Listen and stick.

Sticker time

Monday	Tuesday	Wednesday	Thursday	Friday	Saturday	Sunday

3 Look at 2 and write.

1 On Monday, it's _____ .

2 On Wednesday, it's _____ .

3 On Friday, it's _____ .

4 On Sunday, it's _____ .

4 Play the game.

It's cloudy.

Friday!

Talk buddies

60

I can describe the weather.

1 🎧 ✏️ **Listen and circle.**

It's cool.

It's warm.

It's cold.

🎧 5.6

What's the weather like?
It's warm and sunny.
It's very warm.

2 ✏️ 🎧 5.7 **Look and write. Then listen and number.**

fall   spring   summer   winter

a

b

c

d

It's _____ .   It's _____ .   It's _____ .   It's _____ .

3 💬 **Play Guess the season!**

What's the weather like?

It's cool and windy.

It's fall.

Talk buddies

I can ask and answer about the weather.

61

The kite

1 🎧 **5.8** **Listen and read. What's the weather like?**

① It's very windy!

Oh, no! Look at the kite!

② I can climb the tree!

Thanks, Niko, but the tree is too tall.

I have another idea.

③ Uff! It's heavy. I can't do it. My idea doesn't work.

I have an idea, too!

④ Come on! Let's work together. One, two, three ... Pull!

⑤

Ouch!

But we have our kite! Thanks, Pedro.

Spot!

What can birds eat in the park?

2 ✏️ Read and number the ideas in order.

a make an umbrella ☐   b climb the tree ☐

c move the table ☐   d pull the kite ☐

3 Check (✔). When do they work together?

4 💬 Act out the story.

1 🎧 5.9 💬 **Listen, point, and say. Then play.**

1 fly a kite

2 plant seeds

3 go to the park

4 make snowballs

5 go sledding

6 play indoors

2 🎧 5.10 💬 **Listen and say. Then play in pairs.**

It's rainy and cold.

Play indoors.

What can you do?
It's fall.

fly a kite

It's winter.

make snowballs

Picture Dictionary
page 123

Sing-along

3 🎵 5.11 **Listen, sing, and act.**

It's sunny today. Let's go to the park.
We can ride our bikes and fly our kites!

We can have fun, in the rain or sun!
We can have fun, in the rain or sun!

It's warm today. Let's play in the yard.
We can plant some seeds: carrots and peas!

Chorus

It's rainy today. Let's play indoors.
We can read a book and eat chicken soup!

Chorus

It's snowy today. We can't go to the mall.
Let's go sledding and make snowballs!

Chorus

I can name seasonal activities. >>Extra Lesson>>>>>>>>

Go online Phonics

1 ▶ 🖉 **Watch the video. Write. What season is it?**

In _____ ,
the ants play outside.

🎧 5.12

What do you do in winter?
In winter, we play indoors.

2 🎧 5.13 🖉 **Listen and number. Then ask and answer.**

What do you do in winter?

In winter, we make snowballs.

a

b

c

d

Let's communicate!

3 💬 **Use the cut outs. Play the game.**

What do you do in fall?

In fall, we play indoors.

✂ Cut outs

I can ask and answer about seasonal activities.

Listen and sing. 1.13

Sharing ideas

1 Look and check (✔). Which ideas work?

2 5.14 Listen and say. Which idea do the children like?

3 Check (✔). What can you do when you work with friends?

Say *I don't like your idea.* ◯

Listen to all ideas. ◯

Work together. ◯

Say *Your idea doesn't work.* ◯

Get angry. ◯

Be a hero!

Who do you work together with? Tell a friend.

Relationship skills I can work together with others.

Ant life

1 🎧 5.15 ✏️ **Let's explore! Listen, read, and number.**

underground

team

a Their nests are in the **bark** of trees, **underground**, or under rocks. It's warm in their nests.

b In winter, it's cold. The ants sleep in their nests.

bark

nest

c In summer and fall, ants find food. They eat a lot and their bodies are strong. They work in **teams**. They find leaves and grass to make **nests**.

2 💡 ✏️ **Think Match. What do ants do in summer and in winter?**

1 eat a lot

2 make a nest

3 find food

4 sleep

a summer

b winter

3 ✏️ **Do Check (✔). Where can't ants build a nest?**

 1

 2

 3

 4

 5

I can read and understand about the life of an ant.

My activity tree

Self-management

Let's review

1 ✏️ **Look and write.**

① In _____ , I play soccer.

② In summer, I _____ .

③ In fall, I _____ .

④ In _____ , I make snowballs.

a go to the beach
b fly a kite
c play soccer
d make snowballs

Get ready

2 ✏️ **Read and number in order. Then write.**

Get my things

paper,
_____
_____
_____ ☐

Check
Read and check my spelling. ☐

Show
Show my project to the teacher. ☐

Make
1 Draw my tree.
2 Make the leaves.
3 Write activities on the leaves.
4 Put the leaves on the tree. ☐

Workbook page 61

Create

3 🎨 **Now make your tree. Write.**

Reflect ☹ 🙂 😄

4 **How did I do?**

I plan my project. ◯

I make my project. ◯

I check my project. ◯

I show my project. ◯

I can make and describe an activity tree.

I can do it!

1 🖊️ 🎧 5.16 **Look and write. Then listen and number.**

(cloudy   rainy   snowy   stormy   windy)

 a
 b
 c
 d
 e

_____ _____ _____ _____ _____

2 🖊️ 💬 **Look and write. Then say in pairs.**

(fall   go (x2)   plant   play   spring   summer   winter)

 1
2

3
4

① In _____ , we _____ seeds.

② In _____ , we _____ to the park.

③ In _____ , we _____ indoors.

④ In _____ , we _____ sledding.

Winter!   Go sledding!

3 💡 **Think and check (✔). Then stick!**

I can ...

💬 describe the weather and things I do ◯

📖 read a story ◯

🎵 sing a song ◯

🔧 work together ◯

Sticker time

✔️ **I completed Unit 5!**

6 My day

Video story

go to work

do homework

watch TV

70

1 ▶ 6A **Watch the video. Check (✔). Where does Mom go?**

to a restaurant ◯   to work ◯   to school ◯

2 ▶ 6A ✏ **Watch again. Match. How do they help?**

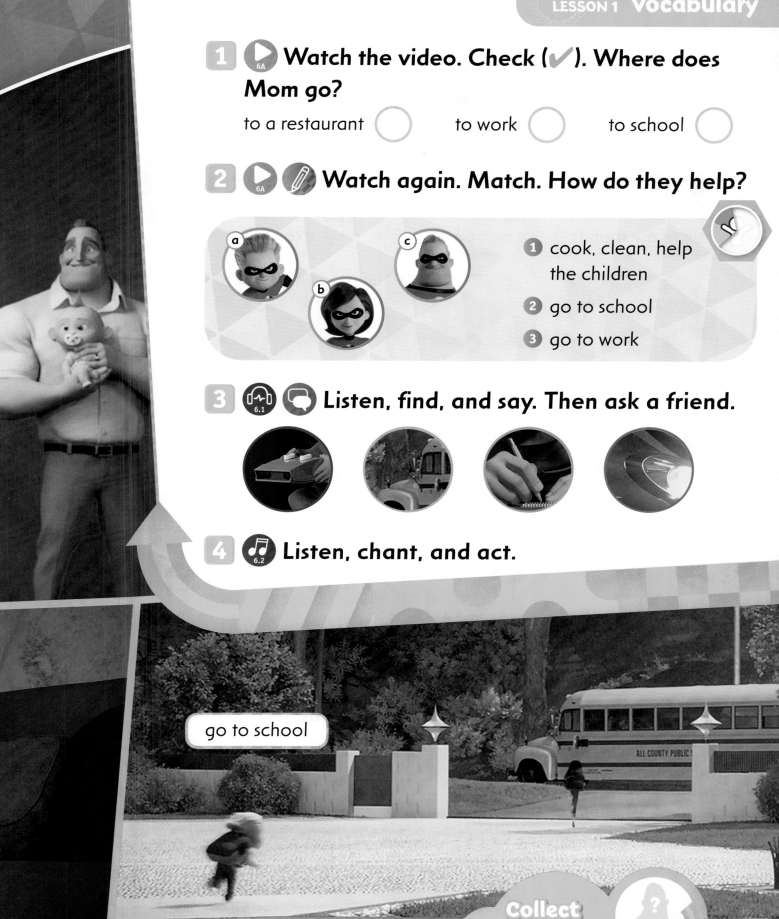

a
b
c

1 cook, clean, help the children
2 go to school
3 go to work

3 🎧 6.1 💬 **Listen, find, and say. Then ask a friend.**

4 🎵 6.2 **Listen, chant, and act.**

go to school

I can name daily routines.

Collect your friend! page 5

71

1 🎧 6.3 💬 **Listen, point, and say. Then play.**

1 talk to my friends

2 come home

3 exercise

4 clean up

5 pack my backpack

6 wash my face

7 go to sleep

8 wake up

2 🎧 6.4 ✏️ **Listen and stick. Then circle.**

Sticker time

1

I exercise /
clean up.

2

I pack my backpack /
go to sleep.

3

I wake up /
wash my face.

3 ✏️ 💬 **Write for you. Then tell a friend.**

wake up _____ _____ _____

_____ _____ _____ go to sleep

I wake up. Then I wash my face.

Talk buddies

I can name daily routines.

1 🖉 **Listen and circle.**

They **talk to their friends /
exercise** at school.

6.6
We watch TV every day.
They have dinner together.
Do you exercise?
Yes, we do./No, we don't.
Do they exercise?
Yes, they do./No, they don't.

2 🎧 **Listen and put a** ✔ **or** ✗ **.**

	watch TV	cook dinner	talk to friends	exercise
Anna and her sister				
Mom and Dad				
me				

3 💬 **Look at 2. Put a** ✔ **or** ✗ **for you. Then ask and answer.**

 Do you watch TV every day?

Yes, I do.

Talk
buddies

I can ask and answer about daily routines.

Let's clean up!

1 🎧 6.8 **Listen and read. Who reads a story to Oscar?**

① Hi, Luiza. Can you come on Wednesday? I go to work at six o'clock.

And I come home at nine o'clock.

Yes, of course. See you then!

Thanks, Luiza!

② On Wednesday …

Do you want to watch TV with us, Amelia?

I can't. I have to do homework.

Would you like some of my chocolate, Amelia?

That's nice of you, Oscar.

③ Hey! Let's help Mom and Dad. Let's clean up the living room.

CLEAN THE HOUSE!

There's a lot to do!

④ We can all help. Then there isn't a lot to do.

Spot!
Can you find Oscar's red shoes?

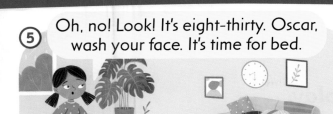

⑤ Oh, no! Look! It's eight-thirty. Oscar, wash your face. It's time for bed.

I can read you a story in bed. Come on!

⑥ At nine o'clock …

Wow! The house is so clean. Thank you, Luiza.

Thank you, Amelia and Oscar, too!

The end

2 ✏️ Read and circle.

1 Mom and Dad go to **school** / **work**.

2 Oscar and Luiza **read a book** / **watch TV**.

3 Oscar goes to bed at **eight-thirty** / **nine o'clock**.

4 Amelia reads a story to **Oscar** / **her parents**.

3 ✏️ Read and match. How do they help the family?

1 clean the house   2 read a story   3 go to work

a

b

c

4 💬 Act out the story.

It's time for bed.

I can read you a story in bed.

Talk buddies

I can read and understand a story.

1 🎧 6.9 💬 **Listen, point, and say. Then play.**

1 in the morning

2 in the afternoon

3 in the evening

4 at night

5 on the weekend

6 on Sundays

📖 Think and write.

the afternoon

in

spring

the morning

Picture Dictionary
page 124

2 🎧 6.10 💬 **Listen and say. Then play in pairs.**

I go to sleep.

Yes!

At night.

Sing-along

3 🎵 6.11 **Listen, sing, and act.**

I wake up in the morning
And I go to school.
I do homework in the afternoon
And I clean up my room.

Every day is the same, work hard through the week.
On Monday to Friday, get up, go to sleep!

We have dinner in the evening,
Then I watch TV.
I go to bed at night
And I go to sleep.

Chorus

On the weekend it's different.
We have fun, fun, fun.
We go to the park
And play games in the sun,
sun, sun!
We go to the park
And play games in the sun,
sun, sun!

I can use simple time expressions. ≫**Extra Lesson**≫≫≫≫≫

Go online Phonics

1 **Watch the video. Check (✔). When does Dash do his math homework?**

in the morning ◯   in the afternoon ◯

6.12

When do you wake up?
I wake up in the morning.
I don't wake up at ten o'clock.

2 **Listen and circle. Then ask and answer.**
6.13

 7:30 = seven-thirty

➊ have breakfast	**7:00 / 7:30**
➋ have lunch	**12:30 / 1:00**
➌ do her homework	in the **afternoon / evening**
➍ ride her bike	**on the weekend / on Mondays**

When do you have breakfast?

Let's communicate!

When do you wake up?

I wake up at 12:30 in the afternoon.

3 **Use the cut outs. Play the game.**

Cut outs

No!

I can ask and answer about daily routines.

♪ 1.13

Listen and sing. ♫

Helping at home

1 💬 **Look and say. How do they help the family?**

2 🎧 6.14 ✏️ **Listen and number. How do they help at home?**

ⓐ

ⓑ

ⓒ

3 💡 💬 **How can you help at home? Write and tell a friend.**

✨ Be a hero! ✨

Make a list of things you can do to help at home.

I can _____ .

That's nice.

Social awareness I can help at home.

Night and day

1 🎧 6.15 ✏️ **Let's explore! Listen, read, and write.**

Earth   Moon   Sun

We live on **Earth**. Earth is big and round. It **spins** around and it doesn't stop. It takes Earth 24 hours to spin around. 24 hours is one day and one night.

It's two o'clock in Mexico City. It's the afternoon and we can see the **Sun**. In Istanbul it's eleven o'clock and it's dark. It's the night and we can see the **Moon**.

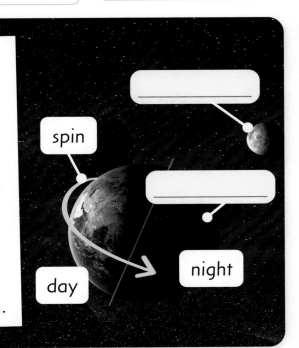

spin

day

night

2 💡 ✏️ **Think Read and write Yes or No.**

➊ The Earth stops at night. _____

➋ There are 24 hours in one day and night. _____

➌ We can't see the Sun when it's dark. _____

➍ We can see the Moon at night. _____

3 ✏️ **Do When can you do this? Look and write day, night, or both.**

_____   _____   _____   _____

I can read and understand about day and night.

My activities clock

Presentation

Let's review

1 🎧 6.16 ✏️ **Look, listen, and write.**

1 We wake up at _____ .

2 We go to school at _____ .

3 We come home at _____ .

4 We go to sleep at _____ .

Get ready

2 🎧 6.17 **Listen and check (✔). What does Lee do this time?**

He speaks slowly. ◯   He speaks fast. ◯

He points at the clock. ◯   He says the times. ◯

Workbook page 73

Create

3 🎨 💬 **Now make your activities clock. Then tell the class.**

Reflect 🙁 🙂 😁

4 **How did I do?**

I say the times. ◯

I say what I do. ◯

I point at the pictures. ◯

I speak slowly. ◯

I can make and present an activities clock.

I can do it!

1 ✏️ 🎧 6.18 **Look and write. Then listen and put a ✔ or ✗.**

do homework
go to school
go to sleep
talk to friends

1 Do they _____ in the morning?

2 Do they _____ at school?

3 Do they _____ at night?

4 Do they _____ in the evening?

2 💬 **Look at 1. Ask and answer for you.**

When do you do homework?

I do homework in the afternoon.

3 💡 **Think and check (✔). Then stick!**

I can ...

💬 talk about daily routines and the time ☐

📖 read a story ☐

🎵 sing a song ☐

🔧 help at home ☐

Sticker time

✔ I completed Unit 6!

Video story

police officer

clerk

baker

1  **Watch the video. Check (✔) the animals you see.**

rabbit ◯   fox ◯   mouse ◯   lion ◯

2 ✏️ **Watch again. Circle.**

Judy's dream is **small** / **big**.

3 🎧 💬 **Listen, find, and say. Then ask a friend.**

4 🎵 **Listen, chant, and act.**

farmer

CARROTS
₩1.20

I can name jobs.

Collect your friend!
page 5

1 🎧 7.3 💬 **Listen, point, and say. Then play.**

1 doctor

2 bus driver

3 architect

4 astronaut

5 athlete

6 vet

7 construction worker

8 firefighter

2 🎧 7.4 ✏️ **Listen and say. Then number.**

ⓐ architect ☐

ⓑ doctor ☐

ⓒ astronaut ☐

ⓓ bus driver ☐

ⓔ vet ☐

ⓕ firefighter ☐

3 ✏️ **Look, read, and write.**

1

I run very fast. I'm an
_____.

2

I'm a doctor for animals.
I'm a _____.

3

I build houses. I'm a
_____
_____.

4 💬 **Play the game.**

Astronaut.

Astronaut, construction worker.

Astronaut, construction worker, vet.

Talk buddies

I can name jobs.

1  **Listen and circle.**

Judy wants to be a
firefighter / **police officer**.

What do you want to be?
I want to be a baker.
She wants to be a police officer.
She doesn't want to be a farmer.

2 **Listen and stick. Then circle.**

Sticker time

1

Nick **wants** / **doesn't want**
to be a construction worker.

2

Nick **wants** / **doesn't want**
to be a police officer.

3

Judy **wants** / **doesn't want**
to be a farmer.

4

She **wants** / **doesn't want** to
be an astronaut.

3 **Play the game.**   What do you want to be?

Amy wants to be a firefighter.

I want to be
a firefighter.

Talk buddies

I can ask and answer about jobs.

85

The firefighter

1 🎧 7.8 **Listen and read. What does Pedro want to be?**

① What do you want to be, Niko?

I want to be an athlete. What about you, Amelia?

I want to be a doctor.

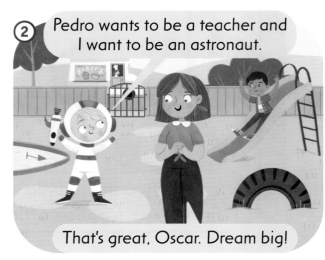

② Pedro wants to be a teacher and I want to be an astronaut.

That's great, Oscar. Dream big!

③ What does Laura want to be?

She wants to be a firefighter.

④ Can a girl be a firefighter, Laura?

Of course! I can show you a picture.

⑤ Oh, no! I can't find a picture of a firefighter, Niko.

Hmm … Come with me!

Spot!
Find a job beginning with the letter "b."

⑥ Look! There's a fire truck!

Ha ha! Yes. That's Aunt Rose.

2 ✏️ Read and match.

1. Niko wants to be
2. Amelia wants to be
3. Oscar wants to be
4. Pedro wants to be
5. Laura wants to be

ⓐ a teacher.
ⓑ a firefighter.
ⓒ an astronaut.
ⓓ an athlete.
ⓔ a doctor.

3 ✏️ Circle. What do they say?

Dream **big** / **small**!

Work / **Play** hard!

4 💬 Act out the story.

Look! There's a fire truck!

Ha ha! Yes.

I can read and understand a story.

1 🎧 7.9 💬 **Listen, point, and say. Then play.**

1 drive

2 bake

3 design

4 build

5 rescue

6 teach

📖 **Think and group.**

People or animals
rescue

Things
build

Picture Dictionary
page 125

2 🎧 7.10 💬 **Listen and say Yes or No. Then play in pairs.**

Firefighters rescue vegetables.   No!

Sing-along

3 🎵 7.11 **Listen, sing, and act.**

What do you do? What do you do?
What do you do all day?

I teach children at school.
I design houses in the town.
I bake cookies and bread.

What do you do? What do you do?
What do you do all day?
Teach, design, bake bread?
What do you do all day?

I build apartment buildings in town.
I rescue people in my truck.
I drive a police car around.

What do you do? What do you do?
What do you do all day?
Build, drive, rescue people?
What do you do all day?

I can say what people do at work.   >>Extra Lesson>>>>>>   Go online Phonics

1  **Watch the video. Circle. What does Gideon do?**

7.12
What does she do?
She's a farmer. She grows vegetables.
She doesn't work at the police station.

2 7.13 **Listen and say. Then match.**

1 Emma

2 Malik

3 Belle

4 Stef

 a

 b

 c

 d

Let's communicate!

3 **Use the cut outs.**
Play the game.

What does he do?

He helps animals.
He's a vet.

 cut outs

I can ask and answer about people's jobs.

Listen and sing. ♫ 1.13

Dreaming big

1 💬 **Look and say. What are their dreams?**

2 🎧 ✏️ **Listen and circle. What's Cam's dream? Why is it hard?**
7.14

I want to be **a teacher** / **an architect**.
It's hard because I can't **draw** / **paint**.

3 💡 ✏️ **Choose and circle or think of your own ideas.**
Then write for you.

My Dream

My name is _____ .
My big dream is to _____
_____ .
I can **work hard** /
dream big / **do it!**

swim with sharks   drive a bus

build a house   design clothes

play soccer   be an astronaut

be a firefighter

⭐ **Be a hero!** ⭐

It's OK to have small
dreams, too. Make a list
of your small dreams.

Self-awareness I can dream big.

Robots at work

1 🎧 7.15 **Let's explore! Listen and read. Where can robots work?**

Robots are **machines**. They help people do their jobs. Some robots are big and strong. They can **lift heavy** things and build houses.

They can do **dangerous** jobs. They can work where people can't work: in the ocean or on the Moon.

Robots can work in factories, too. They can work during the day and at night. They don't feel tired or bored, and they can do the same job many times.

2 💡 **Think Read and put a ✔ or ✗ .**

Same or different?	👨‍🔬	🤖
They can lift heavy things.		
They feel tired.		
They go to sleep at night.		
They can do dangerous jobs.		

3 ✏️ **Do Write. How do these robots help people?**

clean   cook   lift   make cars

I can read and understand about how robots help people.

My dream job poster

Let's review

1 🖊 **Look and write.**

❶ A _____ helps animals.

❷ A _____ works in a hospital.

Get ready

2 🎧 7.16 🖊 **Listen and circle.**

Ollie wants to be a **farmer** / **clerk** / **vet**.
He can **read a book** / **use a computer** /
talk to someone to find out about his dream job.

Workbook page 85

Create

3 🎨 **Now make your poster. Write.**

Reflect ☹ ☺ 😄

4 **How did I do?**

I choose a job. ◯

I find out about the job. ◯

I make my poster. ◯

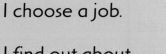

I can make a poster about my dream job.

I can do it!

1 🎧 7.17 ✏️ Listen and number.

 a
 b
 c
 d

2 ✏️ Read and write.

design   drive   rescue   teach

 1
 3
 4

A firefighter
_____
people.

A teacher
_____
at a school.

A bus driver
_____
a bus.

An architect
_____
houses.

3 💡 Think and check (✔). Then stick!

I can ...

💬 name jobs and say
   what people do ☐

📖 read a story ☐

🎵 sing a song ☐

👐 work hard and dream big ☐

Sticker time

☑ **I completed Unit 7!**

8 After school

collect shells

buy ice cream

94

1  Watch the video. Check (✔). Where do Lilo and Stitch go?

park ○

beach ○   mall ○

2 ▶ ✏ Watch again. Circle.

Stitch is **nice** / **mean**.
Lilo is **sad** / **happy**.

3 🎧 💬 Listen, find, and say. Then ask a friend.

4 🎵 Listen, chant, and act.

listen to music

go on a ride

I can name free-time activities.

Collect your friend!

? page 5

1 Listen, point, and say. Then play.

1 do judo

2 surf the internet

3 have a picnic

4 go for a walk

5 bowl

6 take a nap

7 play table tennis

8 do a jigsaw puzzle

2 Listen and stick. Then circle.

Sticker time

1

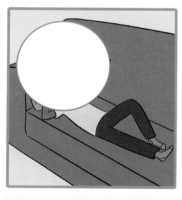

I **have a picnic** / **take a nap**.

2

I **surf the internet** / **do a jigsaw puzzle**.

3

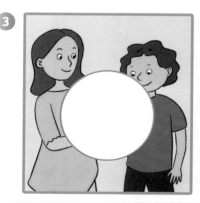

We **bowl** / **play table tennis**.

3 Ask and answer.

Do you do judo?

Yes, I do.

When do you do judo?

I do judo on Mondays.

Talk buddies

I can name free-time activities.

1 🎧 8.5 ✏️ **Listen and circle.**

Lilo and Stitch are
reading / taking a nap.

🎧 8.6

They're reading a book.
They aren't taking a nap.
Are they listening to music?
Yes, they are./No, they aren't.

2 ✏️ 🎧 8.7 **Look, read, and write. Then listen and number.**

bowl   do   have   not listen

ⓐ

They're
_____ .

ⓑ

They aren't
_____
homework.

ⓒ

They _____
_____
a picnic.

ⓓ

They _____
_____
to music.

3 💬 **Look at 2. Ask and answer**

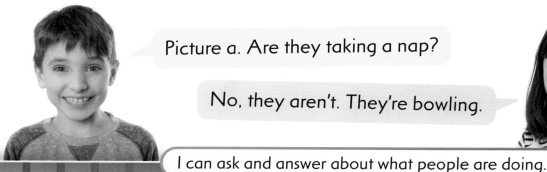

Picture a. Are they taking a nap?

No, they aren't. They're bowling.

Talk
buddies

I can ask and answer about what people are doing.

97

The jigsaw puzzle

1 Listen and read. Why is Oscar sad?

① What are you doing, Amelia?

I'm doing a jigsaw puzzle.

Can I see?

② Yes, look! The kids are collecting shells and the man's buying ice cream.

Oh, yes! And they're taking a nap.

No, they're listening to music. Look!

③ No, they're taking a nap!

No, they aren't. Oh! Please let me do my puzzle!

④ I don't like your puzzle!

Oscar! No! Go away!

⑤ You're mean, Amelia!

Oh, Oscar. Don't cry!

⑥ I'm sorry, Oscar. I feel bad, but you aren't helping me.

Spot!
Can you find an ice cream?

98

2 Read and check (✔). What activities do you see?

collect shells ◯   have a picnic ◯   do a jigsaw puzzle ◯

buy ice cream ◯   do judo ◯   listen to music ◯

3 ✏️ Read and circle. Then number.

1 Amelia feels angry.
She's **nice** / **mean**.

2 Oscar feels **happy** / **sad**.

3 Amelia feels **good** / **bad**.
She's sorry.

a

b

c

4 💬 Act out the story.

Oh, yes! And they're taking a nap.

No, they're listening to music. Look!

Talk buddies

1 8.9 Listen, point, and say. Then play.

1 play tag

2 kick a ball

3 slide

4 swing

5 play hide and seek

6 play in the playground

Alone or with friends?

Alone
swing

With friends
play tag

Picture Dictionary
page 126

2 8.10 Listen and check (✔) in 1. Then play in pairs.

Are you playing tag?

Sing-along

3 8.11 Listen, sing, and act.

Do you want to play in the playground with me?
We can kick a ball.
We can slide and we can swing.

Do you want to play in the playground with me?
Close your eyes.
Let's play hide and seek.

Do you want to play in the playground today?
We can play tag.
Quick! Run away!

I can name playground activities.

>>>Extra Lesson>>>>>>>

Go online
Phonics

1  Watch the video. Circle. Who's rescuing Lilo?

8.12

He's playing hide and seek.
She isn't swinging.
Is he sliding?   Yes, he is./No, he isn't.

2 Look and write *Yes* or *No*. Then cover and tell a friend.

A boy is swinging.

❶ A boy is kicking a ball.   _____
❷ A girl is sliding.   _____
❸ A boy is swinging.   _____
❹ Two boys are playing tag.   _____
❺ A girl is taking a nap.   _____

Let's communicate!

Is Amy sliding?   No, she isn't.

3 Use the cut outs.
Play the game.

Cut outs

I can ask and answer about what people are doing.

Noticing effects of behavior

🎵 1.13 **Listen and sing.**

1 💬 **Look and say. Who's mean? Who feels sad?**

2 🎧 8.13 **Look, listen, and check (✔).**

1 Go away!

ⓐ ○
ⓑ ○

2 I can help you.

ⓐ ○
ⓑ ○

3 💡 ✏️ **Read and draw 😊 or ☹.**

My action		My friend feels ...
I share my ice cream.		→ 😊
I ask you to play.		→ 😊
I kick.		→ 😊

⭐ Be a hero! ⭐

Do you feel bad about something? Make a card to say "I'm sorry."

I'm sorry!

Relationship skills I can notice how my behavior affects others.

How things fly

1 🎧 8.14 **Let's explore! Listen and read.**
What does a plane need to fly?

Birds have **wings**. They use their muscles to move their wings up and down. Air **pressure** lifts them up.

engine

air

wing

pressure

Planes have wings, too. But they don't move up and down. Planes have **engines**. They move the plane forward. The **air** moves over and under the wings. The air pressure over the plane is different from the air pressure under the plane. The air pressure helps lift the plane up.

2 💡 **Think** Read and put a ✔ or ✘.

	moves its wings	has engines	uses air pressure	can fly
a bird				
a plane				

3 ✏️ **Do** How does it fly? Look and write *wings* or *engine*.

1

2

3

4

_____ _____ _____ _____

I can read and understand about how things fly.

My free time poster

Presentation

Let's review

1 🎧 8.15 ✏️ **Listen and number in order. Then match.**

○ I'm playing with my friends.

○ (a) I'm collecting leaves.

○ (b) Millie's swinging

○ (c) Kevin's kicking his ball.

Get ready

2 🎧 8.16 **Listen and check (✔).**

①

②

Workbook page 97

Create

3 🎨 💬 **Now make your poster. Then tell the class.**

Reflect ☹ 🙂 😄

4 **How did I do?**

I make my project. ○

I practice my presentation. ○

I present my poster. ○

I can make and present a poster about my free-time activities.

I can do it!

1   **Listen and number. Then play.**

Take a nap.

One!

 a

 b

 c

 d

 e

 f

2 **Look, read, and write.**

1 Is Lilo singing? _____

2 Are they dancing? _____

3 _____ Stitch _____ the guitar?

4 _____

3 **Think and check (✔). Then stick!**

I can ...

name free-time activities ☐

read a story ☐

sing a song ☐

notice how I make people feel ☐

Sticker time

✔ **I completed Unit 8!**

9 Party time

decorations

1 ▶ **Watch the video. Check (✔).**
Who's the party for?

○ ○ ○

2 ▶ ✏ **Watch again. Write. What's the problem?**

_____ isn't helping. He's eating the _____ .

Video-story

3  Listen, find, and say. Then ask a friend.

4 🎵 Listen, chant, and act.

banner

birthday cake

balloons

I can name party things.

Collect your friend!
page 5

107

1  **Listen, point, and say. Then play.**

1 decorate a cake

2 give a gift

3 blow out candles

4 put up decorations

5 make a card

6 invite friends

7 blow up balloons

8 make goody bags

2  **Listen and stick. Then circle.**

Sticker time

1 Mom is **decorating a cake** / **making a card**.

2 Ava is **giving a gift** / **making goody bags**.

3 Pablo is **blowing out candles** / **blowing up balloons**.

3 **What does your family do for your birthday party? Tell a friend.**

Talk buddies

My mom decorates a cake.

I put up decorations.

I can talk about party preparations.

1 🎧 9.5 ✏️ **Listen and circle.**

They're **reading books** / **singing**.

🎧 9.6

What are you doing?
I'm reading.
What's Anna doing?
She's listening.
What are they doing?
They're singing.

2 🎧 9.7 ✏️ **Listen and number.**

1 Jenny

2 Will

3 Kate

4 Jon

3 💬 **Look at 2. Play *Guess who?***

What are you doing?

You're Jon!

I'm decorating a cake.

Talk buddies

I can ask and answer about what people are doing.

The party

1 🎧 9.8 **Listen and read. Who's the party for?**

① Hi, Niko! Are you getting ready for the party?

Yes, we are. I'm decorating the cake. Come in.

② Dad's in charge.

We still have to decorate the cake, clean the yard, and put up decorations!

Don't worry. We can help.

③ What are Amelia and Oscar doing?

They're cleaning the yard and blowing up balloons.

What's Laura doing?

She's making a banner.

④ Hey, Pedro! Can you help put up the decorations?

⑤ Quick! Luiza comes home at six o'clock.

Yes, of course. Let's work together.

Spot!
Can you find a gift?

110

2 💬 Check (✔) and say. What are they doing?

	🧑	🧑	👧	👧	🧒
decorating a cake					
making a banner					
putting up decorations					
blowing up balloons					
cleaning the yard					

3 ✏️ Read, write, and check (✔).

1 Who's in charge?

_____

2 How many jobs are there?

_____

3 What does Niko help with?

 a   b   c

4 💬 Act out the story.

Wow! Thank you!

It's from *all* of us!

Talk buddies

I can read and understand a story.

1 🎧 9.9 💬 **Listen, point, and say. Then play.**

 **1** watermelon ◯

 **2** popcorn ◯

 **3** party hat ◯

 **4** mask ◯

 **5** lemonade ◯

 **6** candy ◯

📖 Make your own picture dictionary.

party hat

Picture Dictionary
page 127

2 🎧 9.10 💬 **Listen and check (✔) in 1. Then tell a friend.**

 For my party, I have popcorn and watermelons.

Sing-along

3 🎵 9.11 **Listen, sing, and act.**

Popcorn, watermelons, lemonade, and candy.
I'm getting ready for my party!

I'm wearing a mask.
I'm a black and white cat.
And on my head,
There's a green party hat.

Chorus

We're making popcorn
And eating cake.
Let's blow out the candles:
Six, seven, eight!

Chorus

I can name party things.

>>>Extra Lesson>>>>>>>

Go online
Phonics

1 Watch the video. Circle Anna's gifts.

1
2
3

4

It's Anna's dress.
They're Lucas's books.

2 Follow and find. Then ask and answer.

1 Vicky   2 Carlos   3 Cody   4 Ali

What are these?

They're Ali's gifts.

ⓐ    ⓑ    ⓒ    ⓓ

Let's communicate!

3 Use the cut outs. Play the game.

 Cut outs

It's Jun's plane.

They're Nathan's books.

I can say who things belong to.

Listen and sing.
1.13

Sharing tasks

1 💬 **Look and say. Who's in charge? Who helps?**

2 🎧 ✏️ **Listen and circle.**
9.13

1 They're making **party hats** / **masks**.   2 **Tom** / **Emily** is in charge.

3 💡 ✏️ **Look and draw. How can they share the tasks?**

Be a hero!

Are your friends getting ready for something? Is it a big job? Ask how you can help them.

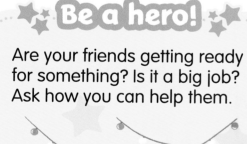

Responsible decision-making I can share tasks in a team.

Rosemaling patterns

1 🎧 9.14 **Let's explore!** Listen and read.
What do you need to make Rosemaling art?

This colorful **pattern** is an example of Rosemaling art. There are a lot of flowers, circles, and lines. You make them with a **paintbrush**. You can put two colors on the paintbrush at the same time.

The patterns are the same on each side of the picture. This is called **symmetry**. To make a pattern, repeat the same shape many times.

symmetry

curvy line

pattern

paintbrush

To make a flower, paint a **curvy** line, a little like a "C" shape. Then paint another "C" shape across from it. Between them, paint an "S" shape.

2 💡 **Think** Read and circle.

1. You make Rosemaling art with **a paintbrush** / **your fingers**.
2. You can put **two** / **three** colors on the paintbrush.
3. Rosemaling art uses a lot of **black** / **curvy** lines.
4. To make a **flower** / **leaf** you paint two "C" shapes.

3 ✏️ **Do** Look and finish the pattern.

I can read and understand about patterns.

My cake design

Self-management

Let's review

1 **Read and circle. Which cake is for May?**

May's favorite color is green, so the cake is green. She doesn't like flowers. She likes balloons. May's seven, so there are seven balloons on the cake.

①
②
③

Get ready

2 **Look and check (✔). Who's ready to work?**

Workbook page 109

Create

3 **Now design your cake. Write.**

Reflect ☹ 🙂 😄

4 **How did I do?**

I know what to do. ◯

I ask for help if I need it. ◯

I make my project. ◯

I do my best. ◯

I can design and describe a birthday cake.

I can do it!

1 ✏️ 💬 Circle and say. What are they doing?

He's **baking** / **making** a card

They're blowing **up** / **out** balloons

He's **putting up** / **giving** a gift

He's **inviting** / **decorating** a cake

2 ✏️ Look and write.

1 they / Olaf / friends _____

2 they / run _____

3 it / Kristoff / paintbrush _____

4 they / make / a banner _____

3 💡 Think and check (✔). Then stick!

I can ...

💬 talk about parties ◯

📖 read a story ◯

🎵 sing a song ◯

🤝 help others and share tasks ◯

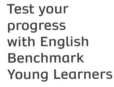

Test your progress with English Benchmark Young Learners

Sticker time

☑️ I completed **Unit 9!**

W

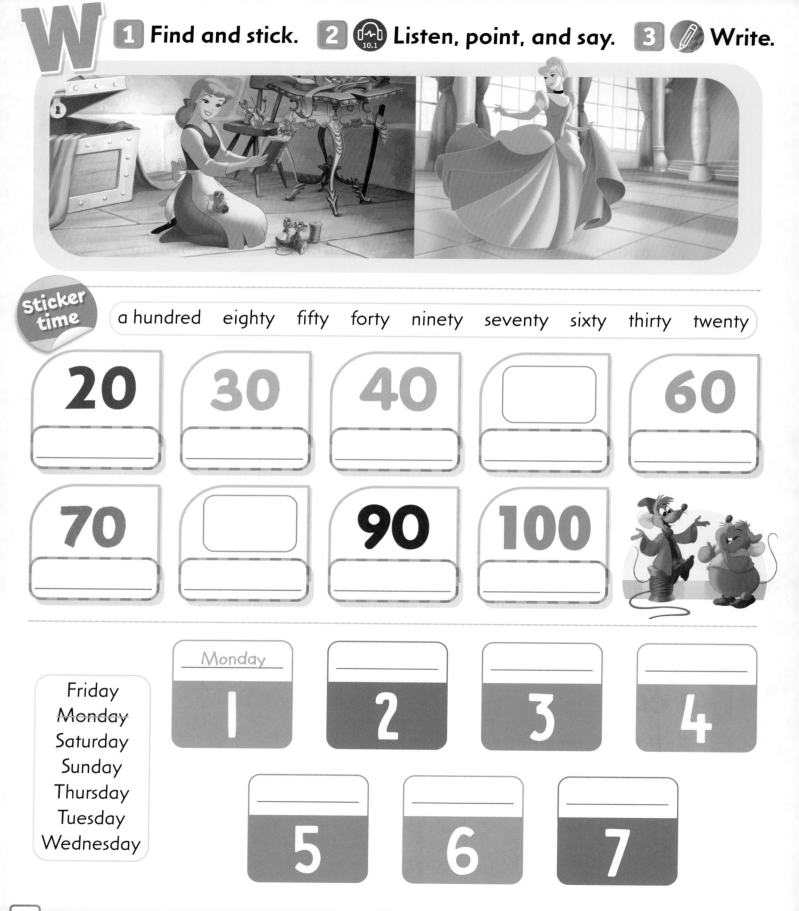

sticker time

a hundred   eighty   fifty   forty   ninety   seventy   sixty   thirty   twenty

20   **30**   **40**   ____   **60**

70   ____   **90**   **100**

Friday
~~Monday~~
Saturday
Sunday
Thursday
Tuesday
Wednesday

Monday
1   **2**   **3**   **4**

5   **6**   **7**

1

1 Find and stick.   **2** Listen, point, and say.   **3** Write.
4 Think and draw.

Sticker time

fast   short
strong   tall

_____

_____

_____

_____

beard   blond   curly
dark   glasses
gray   long   straight

_____

_____

_____

_____

have

_____

_____

_____

_____

_____

_____

cook   horseback ride
play basketball
play the drums
ride a scooter   take pictures

2

1. Find and stick. 2. **10.3** Listen, point, and say. 3. Write.
4. Animals or things? Write.

sticker time

boat   ocean
octopus   shark

beach   crab
dolphin   jellyfish
sea lion   shell
starfish   whale

bucket   sandcastle   sunhat
surfboard   towel   umbrella

animals	things

3

1 Find and stick.   **2** 🎧 10.4 Listen, point, and say.   **3** ✏️ Write.

4 Circle the odd one out.

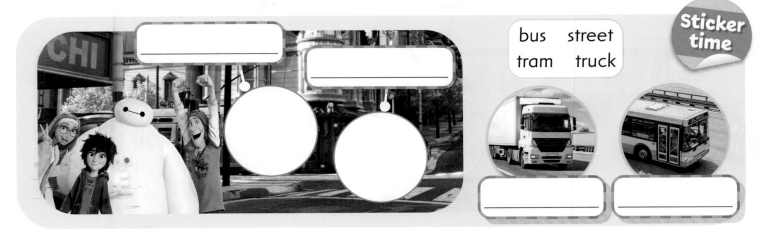

bus   street
tram   truck

Sticker time

_____   _____

bookstore   fire station
grocery store   hospital
movie theater
museum   restaurant
train station

📖

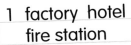

1 factory   hotel
   fire station

2 movie theater
   museum
   hospital

3 mall
   sports center
   grocery store

apartment building
factory   hotel   mall
police station
sports center

4

1 Find and stick. **2** Listen, point, and say. **3** ✏️ Write.

4 What food do you eat?

cake peas potatoes soup

Sticker time

_____

_____

_____

_____

_____

_____

chicken chocolate
kiwis lemons
mangoes nuts
pineapples yogurt

_____

_____

_____

_____

_____

_____

_____

_____

breakfast burger cereal
dinner fries lunch

_____

_____

_____

_____

_____

_____

breakfast   dinner
        lunch

5

1 Find and stick. **2** Listen, point, and say. **3** Write.

4 What can you do?

fall   spring   summer   winter

Sticker time

cloudy   cool   rainy
snowy   stormy
sunny   warm   windy

It's hot.

_____

_____

It's cold.

_____

_____

fly a kite   go sledding
go to the park
make snowballs
plant seeds   play indoors

123

6

1 Find and stick. **2** Listen, point, and say. **3** Write.

4 In, on, or at?

do homework   go to school   go to work   watch TV

_____   _____   _____   _____

come home   clean up   exercise   go to sleep
pack my backpack   talk to my friends   wake up   wash my face

_____   _____   _____   _____

_____   _____   _____   _____

_____   _____   _____

at night   in the afternoon
in the evening   in the morning
on Sundays   on the weekend

 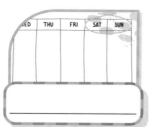 

_____   _____   _____

in   on   at

7

1 Find and stick. **2** Listen, point, and say. **3** Write.

4 Think and group.

baker   clerk   farmer   police officer

Sticker time

_____   _____   _____   _____

architect   astronaut   athlete   bus driver   construction worker
doctor   firefighter   vet

_____   _____   _____   _____

_____   _____   _____   _____

_____   _____   _____

_____   _____   _____

help/rescue	design/make

bake   build   design
drive   rescue   teach

125

8

1 Find and stick. **2** 🎧 10.9 Listen, point, and say. **3** ✏️ Write.
4 Circle activities you do at home. Then write two more.

buy ice cream   collect shells
go on a ride   listen to music

sticker time

bowl   do a jigsaw puzzle   do judo   go for a walk   have a picnic
play table tennis   surf the internet   take a nap

kick a ball   play hide and seek
play in the playground
play tag   slide   swing

9

1 Find and stick. **2** 🎧 10.10 Listen, point, and say. **3** ✏️ Write.
4 Circle things for your party. Then draw one more.

balloons   banner
birthday cake   decorations

Sticker time

blow out candles   blow up balloons   decorate a cake   give a gift
invite friends   make a card   make goody bags   put up decorations

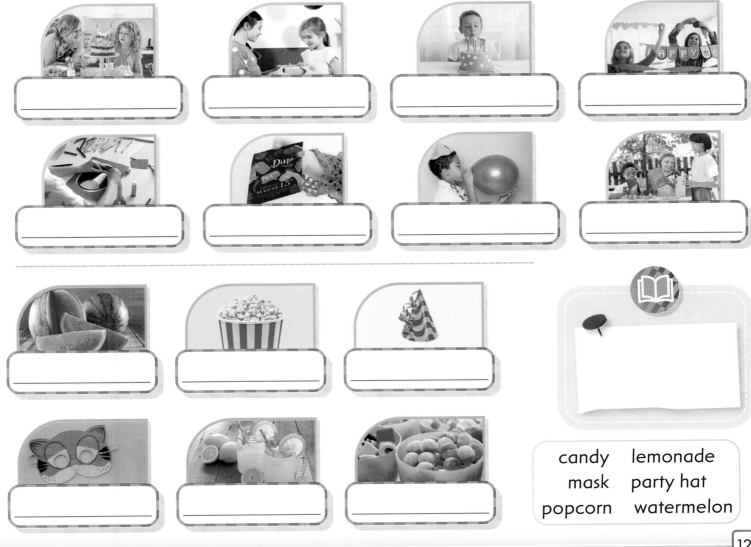

candy   lemonade
mask   party hat
popcorn   watermelon

Pearson Education Limited
KAO Two
KAO Park
Hockham Way
Harlow, Essex
CM17 9SR
England
and Associated Companies throughout the world.

pearsonenglish.com

First published 2022
ISBN: 978-1-292-44157-3
Set in Arta Medium 19/25pt

Printed in Slovakia by Neografia

Acknowledgements
The publishers and authors would like to thank the following people for their feedback and comments during the development of the material: Dilek Akin, Burcu Hasbay, Martha Illescas, Maja Jankovic, Sandy Meza, Monica Medina, Olga Mokrushina, Soledad O'Keefe, Anita Parlaj.

Unit 1

Unit 2

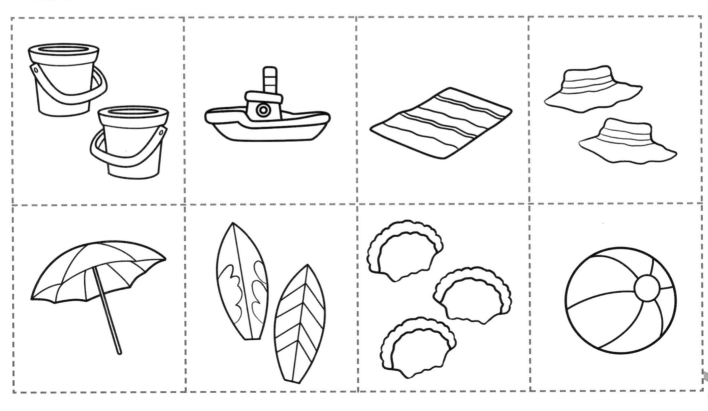

Unit 3

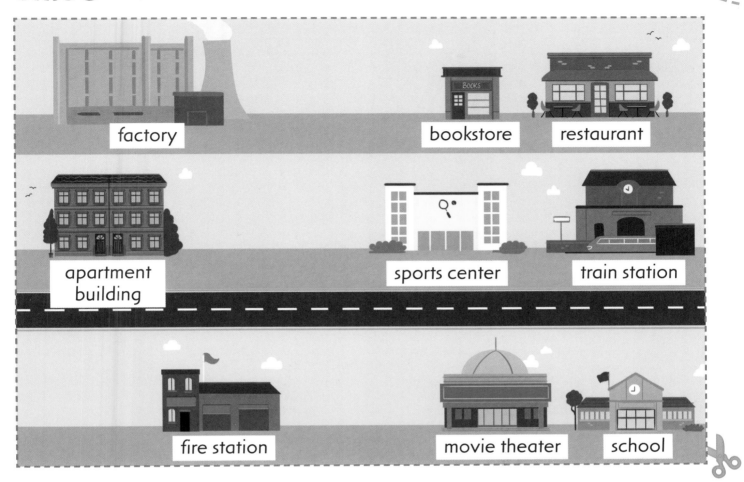

factory

bookstore

restaurant

apartment building

sports center

train station

fire station

movie theater

school

museum

grocery store

mall

hotel

hospital

police station

Unit 4

Menu

Unit 5

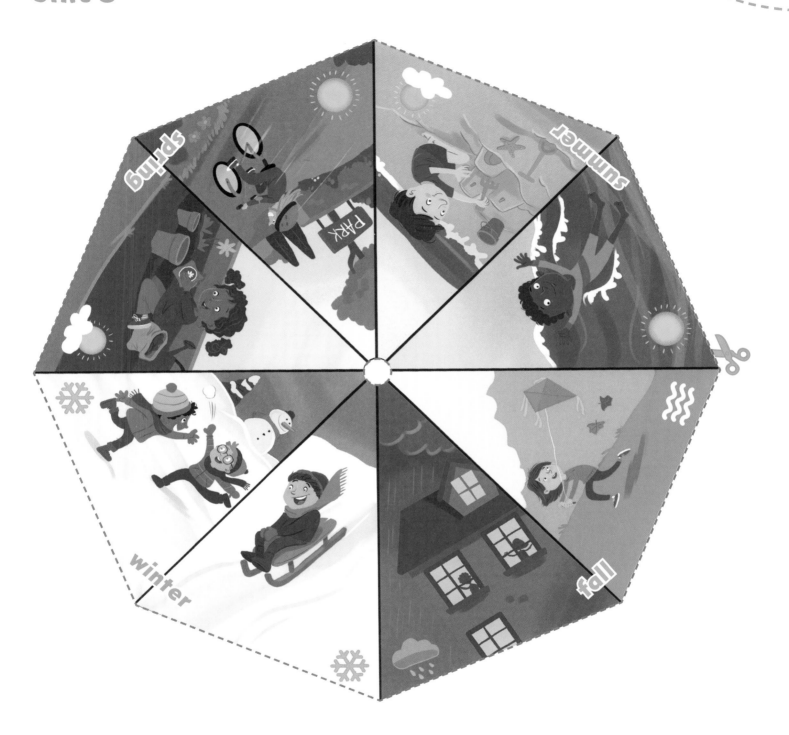

Unit 6

at night

in the afternoon

in the morning

in the evening

in the morning

in the afternoon

Unit 7

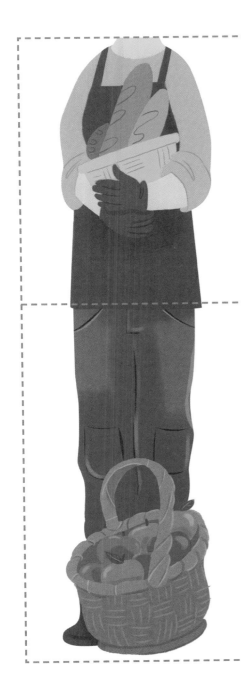

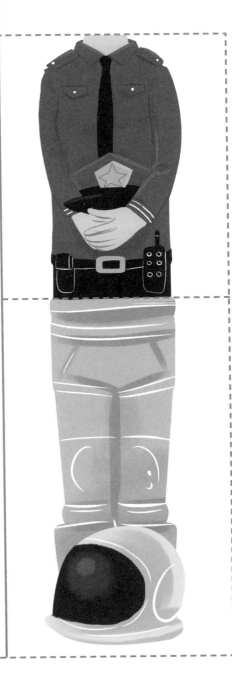

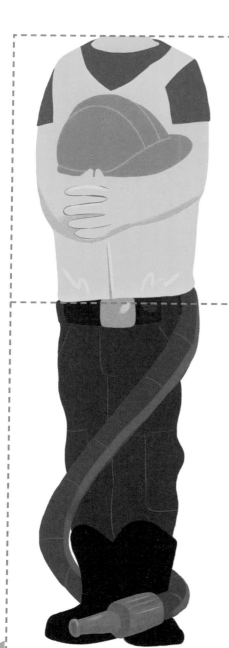

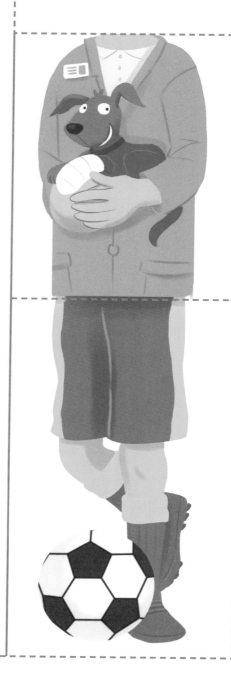

Unit 8

Ben

Sam

Lin

Mei

Eva

Amy

Unit 9

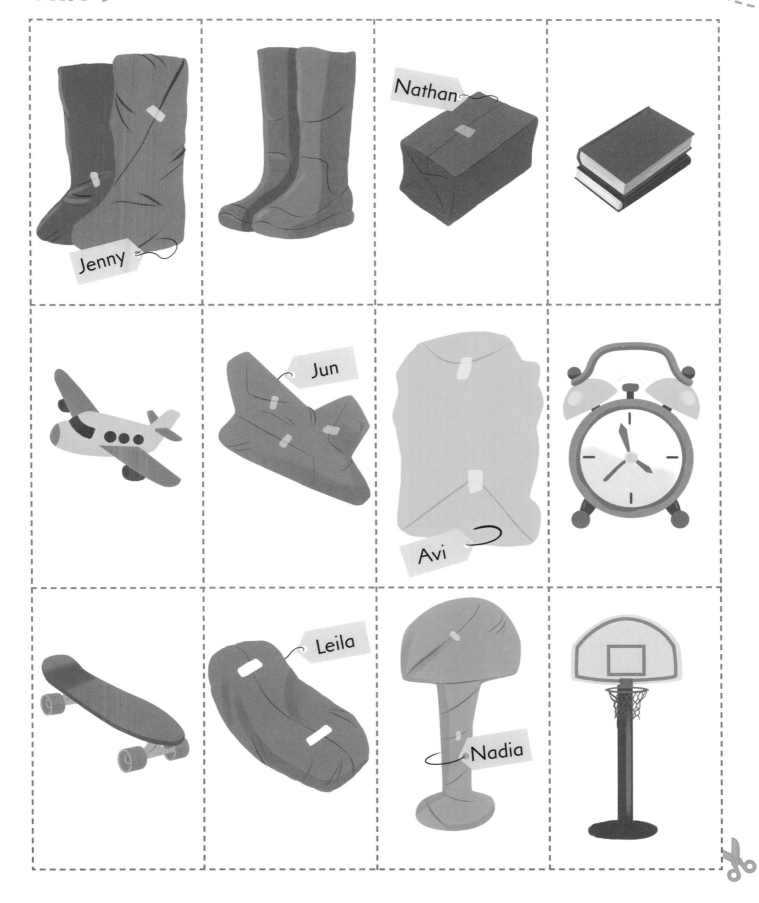

Welcome

50
80

Unit 1

Unit 2

Unit 3

Unit 4

Unit 5

Unit 6

Unit 7

Unit 8

Unit 9